OXFORD BOOKWORMS LIBRARY
*Thriller & Adventure*

# Goodbye, Mr Hollywood

Stage 1 (400 headwords)

Series Editor: Jennifer Bassett
Founder Editor: Tricia Hedge
Activities Editors: Jennifer Bassett and Alison Baxter

JOHN ESCOTT

# Goodbye,
# Mr Hollywood

OXFORD UNIVERSITY PRESS

# OXFORD
## UNIVERSITY PRESS

Great Clarendon Street, Oxford OX2 6DP

Oxford University Press is a department of the University of Oxford
It furthers the University's objective of excellence in research, scholarship,
and education by publishing worldwide in

Oxford New York

Auckland Bangkok Buenos Aires Cape Town Chennai
Dar es Salaam Delhi Hong Kong Istanbul Karachi Kolkata
Kuala Lumpur Madrid Melbourne Mexico City Mumbai Nairobi
São Paulo Shanghai Taipei Tokyo Toronto

Oxford and Oxford English are registered trade marks of
Oxford University Press in the UK and in certain other countries

ISBN 0 19 422942 4

Seventh impression 2003

First published in Oxford Bookworms 1997
This second edition published in the Oxford Bookworms Library 2000

A complete recording (in American English) of this Bookworms edition of
*Goodbye, Mr Hollywood*
is available on cassette ISBN 0 19 422859 2

Illustrated by Paul Dickinson

Printed in Spain by Unigraf s.l.

# CONTENTS

STORY INTRODUCTION                         i

1  Mystery girl                            1

2  A hand in the back                      9

3  A walk in the park                      14

4  The man with white hair                 18

5  Vancouver Island                        22

6  A tea party                             28

7  At the police station                   34

8  A nice smile                            39


GLOSSARY                                   41

ACTIVITIES: Before Reading                 44

ACTIVITIES: While Reading                  45

ACTIVITIES: After Reading                  48

ABOUT THE AUTHOR                           52

ABOUT BOOKWORMS                            53

# — 1 —

## Mystery girl

It all began on a beautiful spring morning in a village called Whistler, in Canada – a pretty little village in the mountains of British Columbia.

There was a café in the village, with tables outside, and at one of these tables sat a young man. He finished his breakfast, drank his coffee, looked up into the blue sky, and felt the warm sun on his face. Nick Lortz was a happy man.

The waiter came up to his table. 'More coffee?' he asked.

'Yeah. Great,' said Nick. He gave the waiter his coffee cup.

The waiter looked at the camera on the table. 'On vacation?' he said. 'Where are you from?'

'On vacation?'

'San Francisco,' Nick said. He laughed. 'But I'm not on vacation – I'm working. I'm a travel writer, and I'm doing a book on mountains in North America. I've got some great pictures of your mountain.'

The two men looked up at Whistler Mountain behind the village. It looked very beautiful in the morning sun.

'Do you travel a lot, then?' asked the waiter.

'All the time,' Nick said. 'I write books, and I write for travel magazines. I write about everything – different countries, towns, villages, rivers, mountains, people . . .'

The waiter looked over Nick's head. 'There's a girl across the street,' he said. 'Do you know her?'

Nick turned his head and looked. 'No, I don't.'

'Well, she knows you, I think,' the waiter said. 'She's watching you very carefully.' He gave Nick a smile. 'Have a nice day!' He went away, back into the café.

Nick looked at the girl across the street. She was about twenty-five, and she was very pretty. 'She *is* watching me,' Nick thought. Then the girl turned and looked in one of the shop windows. After a second or two, she looked back at Nick again.

Nick watched her. 'She looks worried,' he thought. 'What's she doing? Is she waiting for somebody?'

Suddenly, the girl smiled. Then she walked across the street, came up to Nick's table, and sat down. She put her bag down on the table. The bag was half-open.

2

*The girl came up to Nick's table.*

'Hi! I'm Jan,' she said. 'Do you remember me? We met at a party in Toronto.'

'Hi, Jan,' said Nick. He smiled. 'I'm Nick. But we didn't meet at a party in Toronto. I don't go to parties very often, and never in Toronto.'

3

'Oh,' the girl said. But she didn't get up or move away.

'Have some coffee,' said Nick. The story about the party in Toronto wasn't true, but it was a beautiful morning, and she was a pretty girl. 'Maybe it was a party in Montréal. Or New York.'

The girl laughed. 'OK. Maybe it was. And yes, I'd love some coffee.'

When she had her coffee, Nick asked, 'What are you doing in Whistler? Or do you live here?'

'Oh no,' she said. 'I'm just, er, just travelling through. And what are *you* doing here?'

'I'm a travel writer,' Nick said, 'and I'm writing a book about famous mountains.'

'That's interesting,' she said. But her face was worried, not interested, and she looked across the road again.

A man with very short, white hair walked across the road. He was about sixty years old, and he was tall and thin. The girl watched him.

'Are you waiting for someone?' asked Nick.

'No,' she said quickly. Then she asked, 'Where are you going next, Nick?'

'To Vancouver, for three or four days,' he said.

'When are you going?' she asked.

'Later this morning,' he said. There was a letter in the top of the girl's half-open bag. Nick could see some of the writing, and he read it because he saw the word

'Vancouver' – . . . *and we can meet at the Empress Hotel,
Victoria, Vancouver Island, on Friday afternoon . . .*

'So she's going to Vancouver too,' he thought.

Suddenly the girl said, 'Do you like movies?'

'Movies? Yes, I love movies,' he said. 'Why?'

'I know a man, and he – he loves movies, and going to
the cinema,' she said slowly. 'People call him "Mr

*'Are you waiting for someone?' asked Nick.*

Hollywood".' She smiled at Nick. 'Can I call you "Mr Hollywood" too?'

Nick laughed. 'OK,' he said. 'And what can I call you?'

She smiled again. 'Call me Mystery Girl,' she said.

'That's a good name for you,' said Nick.

Just then, the man with white hair came into the café. He did not look at Nick or the girl, but he sat at a table near them. He asked the waiter for some breakfast, then he began to read a magazine.

The girl looked at the man, then quickly looked away again.

'Do you know him?' Nick asked her.

'No,' she said. She finished her coffee quickly and got up. 'I must go now,' she said.

Nick stood up, too. 'Nice to—' he began.

But the girl suddenly took his face between her hands, and kissed him on the mouth. 'Drive carefully, Mr Hollywood. Goodbye,' she said, with a big, beautiful smile. Then she turned and walked quickly away.

Nick sat down again and watched her. She walked down the road and into a big hotel.

'Now what,' thought Nick, 'was *that* all about?'

\*   \*   \*

The man with white hair watched Nick and waited. After four or five minutes, Nick finished his coffee, took his books and his camera, and left the café. His car was just outside

*'Drive carefully, Mr Hollywood.'*

the girl's hotel, and he walked slowly along the street to it.

The man with white hair waited a second, then quickly followed Nick.

From a window high up in the hotel, the girl looked down into the road. She saw Nick, and the man with white hair about fifty yards behind him. Nick got into his car, and the man with white hair walked quickly to a red car across the street. Five seconds later Nick drove away in his blue car, and the red car began to follow him.

When the girl saw this, she smiled, then went to put some things in her travel bag.

*The man with white hair walked quickly*
*to a red car across the street.*

## — 2 —

## A hand in the back

That evening, in his hotel room in Vancouver, Nick could not stop thinking about the girl in the Whistler café. Why did she come and sit with him? She didn't know him, and that story about a party in Toronto wasn't true. And she was worried about something. But what?

And that kiss! It was nice, of course, but why did she do it? 'Maybe she liked my face,' Nick thought. 'Or my brown eyes. But I'm not going to see her again, so it doesn't matter. Forget it.'

He put some money in his pocket and went downstairs to the hotel restaurant. But there were no free tables, so he walked down to Gastown and found a restaurant there.

After dinner, he went for a walk. Vancouver was a friendly city, and Nick liked walking through Gastown and Chinatown, looking in the shops and watching the people. It was nearly dark now, and it was a busy time of the evening. There were a lot of cars, and a lot of people.

After a time, Nick began to walk back to his hotel. He came to a busy street, and waited, with a small crowd of people, to go across. A tall woman in a blue dress stood next to him. She turned and smiled at him.

'It's the first warm evening of spring,' she said. 'It's nice to be out, after the long cold winter.'

'Yeah,' said Nick. 'It's great. It's—'

Suddenly, there was a hand in his back – and the hand pushed Nick into the road. Nick fell on his face, in front of a big green car.

People screamed.

But the green car stopped, only inches from Nick's head. The woman in the blue dress ran into the road and pulled Nick to his feet.

'Are you OK? What happened?' she said.

The driver of the green car shouted angrily at Nick, but Nick did not hear him.

*Nick fell on his face, in front of a big green car.*

'Somebody pushed me,' he said to the woman. 'I didn't fall – somebody pushed me!'

'Pushed you?' said the woman. 'Who? I didn't see anybody.'

Nick looked at the faces of the people near him, but he didn't know them.

Then he saw a man's back. The man was tall and thin, and had very short white hair. He walked quickly away down the street, and did not look back.

'Hey, you!' Nick shouted. 'Wait!'

But the man did not stop, and he was soon lost in the crowds.

'Did *he* push you?' asked the woman in the blue dress.

11

'I . . . I don't know,' Nick said.

'Do you know him?' she asked.

'I don't know his name,' Nick said. 'But I know that short white hair. Now where did I see it before?'

The woman began to move away. 'I must get home,' she said. 'Are you OK now?'

'Yeah, I'm OK,' Nick said. 'And thanks. Thanks for your help.'

'That's OK.' The woman smiled. 'Be careful now!'

\* \* \*

Back in his hotel, Nick sat on his bed and thought. 'It was an accident. Nobody pushed me, it was an accident. Nobody wants to kill me. And there are hundreds of men in Vancouver with white hair.'

It was one o'clock in the morning, but Nick couldn't sleep. He listened to the cars in the road, and he looked at the night sky through his hotel room window.

Then he sat at the table and tried to write some more of his book about mountains, but he couldn't think about his work. He got back into bed.

There were four or five magazines in the hotel room. They were not very interesting, but Nick sat in bed and opened one . . . *and saw a photo of 'Mystery Girl'!*

He looked at the picture very carefully. But, yes, it was her! Jan, the girl from the Whistler café.

She was next to a man of about fifty or fifty-five, and

*Nick sat in bed and opened one . . .* and saw a photo of
'Mystery Girl'!

they were in the garden of a big, expensive house. They
smiled at the camera, and they looked very happy.

*Canadian millionaire, Howard Hutson, and his
daughter, Meg*, it said under the picture, *at their home in
Toronto*. Meg Hutson! Not Jan. Not Mystery Girl. Meg
Hutson, the daughter of a millionaire! Nick read it again.

'Why did she come and sit with *me* in the café at
Whistler?' he thought. 'Millionaires' daughters don't sit

13

with strangers in cafés, and then give them a big kiss when they leave! Why did she do it? What did she want?'

\* \* \*

He thought back to the café in Whistler, and the girl next to him at the table. Then he remembered something. He remembered a man at a table near them in the café. A tall thin man, about sixty years old. A man with very short white hair.

Nick didn't sleep much that night.

— **3** —

## A walk in the park

The next day was Thursday. Nick stayed in his hotel room and wrote about mountains all morning. Then he drove to Stanley Park in the afternoon. He sat and read a book for an hour, then he went for a walk under the tall trees.

There was nobody here. It was quiet, and he could walk and think. He thought about Meg Hutson, and about the man with white hair. Did he know Meg Hutson? Did she know him? He remembered Meg Hutson's last words. *Drive carefully, Mr Hollywood.*

Why did she say that? Why did she call him Mr Hollywood? He didn't understand any of it.

Suddenly, he heard a noise.

*Nick turned and ran.*

He stopped. 'That was a gun!' he thought. 'There's somebody in the trees with a gun! There it is again!'

Then something hit the tree over his head.

'Somebody's shooting at me!' Nick thought. He turned and ran.

And somebody began to run after him.

Nick ran through the trees. There was no sun in here, and it was half-dark. And there were no people. Nobody to help him.

'I must get to my car,' Nick thought. 'Find some people . . . the police . . .' He ran on.

He could still hear the gunman behind him, so he ran faster. After three or four minutes, he stopped and listened.

Nothing. It was all quiet.

Nick was afraid. 'What's happening?' he thought. 'Why is somebody shooting at me? First a hand pushes me in front of a car, and now somebody's shooting at me!'

He waited another second or two, then walked quickly back to his car. He was very careful. He looked and listened all the time. But nobody came out of the trees, and nobody shot at him. Then he saw people – women with young children, some boys with a football, two men with a dog. He began to feel better. 'Nobody can shoot me now,' he thought. 'Not with all these people here.'

Ten minutes later, he was back at his car.

There was a letter on the window. Nick read it. It said: *I'm going to kill you, Mr Hollywood.*

\*    \*    \*

Nick drove to the nearest police station. He waited for half an hour, then a tired young policeman took him into a small room. Nick told his story, and the policeman wrote it all down.

16

*'How many people are there in this town with guns?'*

'So what are you going to do?' asked Nick.

'Nothing,' said the policeman.

'Nothing!' said Nick. 'But somebody shot at me, and—'

'Mr Lortz,' the policeman said tiredly. 'How many people are there in this town with guns?'

'I don't know,' said Nick. 'But . . .'

'You didn't see the gunman. Was it a man, a boy, a woman? Colour of eyes? Long hair, short hair? You don't know, because you didn't see anybody. Maybe it was an

17

old girlfriend. Maybe somebody doesn't like your travel books, Mr Lortz.'

'But what about the man with white hair in Whistler?' said Nick. 'The girl, Meg Hutson, called me Mr Hollywood in the café, and this man heard her. And now I get a letter to Mr Hollywood on *my* car. Who *is* this Mr Hollywood?'

'We all want answers to our questions, Mr Lortz,' the policeman said, 'but we don't always get them.'

Questions. But no answers.

Nick walked out of the police station and drove to his hotel. He was angry, and afraid.

'How did the man with white hair find me in Vancouver?' he thought. 'Did he follow me from Whistler? Is he following me now? Maybe he's staying at my hotel, too. In the next room. With his gun.'

— **4** —

## The man with white hair

Nick stopped his car in front of the hotel. He looked carefully before he got out, but there was nobody with white hair near the hotel.

He half-ran through the hotel doors and went to the desk inside.

'I'm looking for a man with very short white hair,' he

*'It's very important. Please help me!'*

said to the woman behind the desk. 'He's staying here, I think. He's about sixty years old, and he's tall and thin.'

The woman did not look very interested. 'There are a lot of visitors in the hotel,' she said. 'Do you know his name?'

'No, I don't,' Nick said. 'He's, er, a friend of a friend, you see. He arrived in Vancouver yesterday, and I must find him. It's very important. Please help me!'

The woman looked at him. 'There are three hundred and fifty rooms in this hotel,' she said, 'and maybe thirty or forty men with white hair. How can I remember all their

19

names?' She turned away to answer a telephone call.

Nick walked away from the desk.

'A drink,' he thought. 'I need a drink.' He went into the hotel bar, got a drink and sat down at a table.

'So what do I do now?' he thought.

And then he remembered something. A letter in the girl's half-open bag in the Whistler café.

*. . . and we can meet at the Empress Hotel, Victoria, Vancouver Island, on Friday afternoon . . .*

And tomorrow was Friday.

'I'm going to Victoria, on Vancouver Island!' he thought. 'To the Empress Hotel!'

\* \* \*

*The boy and Nick fell down on the floor.*

20

Nick had dinner in the hotel that evening. He finished eating and got up from his table . . . *and saw the man with white hair.*

Nick moved quickly. The man was at the hotel desk. Nick could see the white head above the other heads near the desk.

'Excuse me!' said Nick. He pushed past the people in the hotel restaurant. A small boy ran in front of him and Nick ran into him. The boy and Nick fell down on the floor. The boy began to cry.

'Hey!' said a woman behind Nick.

'I'm very sorry!' said Nick. He got up and helped the

21

boy to his feet. 'Are you OK?' he asked the boy.

'Be more careful next time,' said the woman.

Nick moved away quickly, but when he looked back at the hotel desk, he couldn't see the man with white hair. He pushed through the crowd of people.

'That man!' he shouted at the woman behind the desk. 'That man with short white hair. Where did he go?'

The woman looked at Nick. 'Mr Vickers?' she said. 'I don't know.'

'Vickers? Is that his name?' said Nick. 'What's his room number?'

'I'm sorry, I can't tell you that,' the woman said.

'But I need to—' began Nick.

The woman turned away to answer the telephone.

After a second or two, Nick went upstairs to his room.

'Vickers,' he thought. 'Does Meg Hutson know Mr Vickers? I need some answers, and I need them quickly!'

— **5** —

## Vancouver Island

Tsawwassen was about twenty-three miles south of Vancouver. Nick drove there in his car the next morning for the one o'clock ferry to Vancouver Island. Every five minutes, he looked behind him. The road was busy – black

22

cars, white cars, red cars, green cars. Maybe Vickers was in one of them.

At Tsawwassen Nick drove his car on to the ferry. There were a lot of cars and crowds of people. Nick got out of his car and walked up and down the ship. He looked for a man with white hair but he didn't see one.

*He looked for a man with white hair but he didn't see one.*

Soon the ferry began to move and Nick felt better. He found the ferry restaurant and got something to eat. More people came in. Nick looked at the faces of all the older men. Some had hats on, so he looked for somebody tall and thin, but there was nobody.

'Maybe he's not on the ferry,' Nick thought. 'Maybe he's back in Vancouver.'

Later, Nick walked around the ship again. Once, he thought he saw the man with white hair in the crowds, but he could not be sure.

Ninety minutes after leaving Tsawwassen, the ferry arrived at Swartz Bay on Vancouver Island, and Nick went back down to his car.

Swartz Bay was twenty miles north of Victoria. Nick drove quickly, and again, looked behind him every four or five minutes. Once, he saw a red car about two hundred yards behind him.

'Did I see that car on the road from Vancouver to Tsawwassen?' he thought.

He drove more slowly, but the red car still stayed two hundred yards behind him, and Nick couldn't see the driver's face or hair.

Soon he was in the busy streets of Victoria, and Nick didn't see the red car behind him again.

Victoria was a city of gardens and beautiful old buildings. Nick liked Victoria very much, but today he

*'This is her.'*

wasn't interested in gardens or buildings.

He found the Empress Hotel, went inside and walked across to the desk.

'Can I help you?' a young man asked Nick.

'I'm meeting a friend here this afternoon,' said Nick. 'Miss Hutson.'

'Hutson?' said the young man. 'Wait a minute.' He went away and came back. 'Sorry, but there's no Miss Hutson staying here.'

Nick took something from his pocket. It was the photograph of Meg and her father, from the magazine. 'This is her,' he said.

The young man looked at the picture. 'Oh, right. You mean Howard Hutson's daughter,' he said. 'She's not staying here, but I saw her ten or fifteen minutes ago. She was with somebody – a man. He asked me about the tea room.'

'The tea room?' said Nick. 'Where's that?'

\* \* \*

The man with short white hair was tired. He couldn't sleep and he couldn't eat. He thought about only one thing, all the time. He drove and he watched, and he waited and he followed.

When he drove into Victoria, the streets were busy, and suddenly he lost the blue car in front of him. Angrily, he drove around the city, past all the big hotels. 'I must find him,' he said. 'I must do it. Today.'

Then he saw the Empress Hotel, and in the street outside it, a blue car.

He drove past the hotel, left his car, and ran back down the street. He went across the road and walked past the downstairs windows. There was a big room with tables and chairs, and a lot of people. He looked carefully at all the faces.

'There she is!' he said suddenly.

There were two men with the girl. He couldn't see their faces, only the backs of their heads, but one of the men was in a green shirt.

'Mr Hollywood,' the man said, and smiled. 'Goodbye, Mr Hollywood.' People in the street turned to look at him, but the man did not see them.

He walked up to the doors of the hotel and put a hand into his pocket. Inside, the gun was cold and hard.

*'Goodbye, Mr Hollywood.'*

27

# — 6 —

## A tea party

Nick looked through the doors of the tea room in the Empress Hotel.

Meg Hutson sat at a table with a man. The man was about thirty, or maybe a year or two younger. He was tall, and brown from the sun. He wore a white shirt, white

*Meg Hutson sat at a table with a man.*

trousers, and white shoes. He said something to Meg, and she laughed. She looked very happy.

A waiter came up to Nick. 'Can I get you some tea?' he asked.

'No, thanks,' said Nick. 'I'm with the two people over there.' And he walked across to Meg's table.

'Hello, Mystery Girl,' said Nick. 'Remember me? We met at Whistler. Your name was Jan then. But maybe today it's Meg Hutson.'

Meg Hutson looked up at him. 'Oh,' she said, and her face went red.

'Who is this, Meg?' asked the man.

'This is Nick,' said Meg. 'He's a writer. Nick, this is Craig Winters.'

'Sometimes called Mr Hollywood?' said Nick.

'Maybe. But how did *you* know that?' asked Craig Winters.

'I guessed,' said Nick. 'And I think I'm beginning to understand. Can I ask you a question, Mr Winters? Does somebody want to kill you?'

Craig Winters' face went white. 'Kill me?'

'What are you talking about?' asked Meg.

'Before I tell you, answer this question, please,' said Nick. 'You called *me* Mr Hollywood in Whistler. And you wanted the man at the next table, the man with white hair, to hear you. Is that right?'

29

*'I wanted him to follow you, and not me.'*

Meg Hutson did not answer at first. Then she said quietly, 'Yes.'

'Why?' asked Nick.

'I wanted him to follow you, and not me.'

'Why?' Nick asked again.

'I think he's a detective,' said Meg. 'And I think he's working for my father. I saw him soon after I left Toronto. He followed me.' Meg put her hand on Craig Winters' arm.

'My father doesn't like Craig. A month ago, he told me not to see Craig again. I'm not happy, and he knows that. I think he guessed that I'm meeting Craig. And now he wants to find Craig and stop him seeing me.'

'Stop him?' said Nick. 'Or kill him?'

'No!' Meg Hutson said. 'Daddy doesn't—'

'The man with white hair pushed me in front of a car in Vancouver,' Nick told her. 'And he shot at me in Stanley Park.'

'What!' said Meg.

'Tell – tell me about this man with white hair,' Winters said suddenly.

Nick looked at him. 'He's about sixty, and he's tall and thin,' he said.

'Do you know his name?' asked Winters.

'Vickers,' said Nick.

Craig Winters suddenly looked ill. 'Did he – did he follow you to Victoria? Did he follow you here?'

'I don't know,' said Nick. He watched Winters. 'You're afraid of him. Why? Why does this man Vickers want to kill you, Winters?'

Before Craig Winters could answer, Meg's face went white. 'Oh, no!' she said. 'Look! Look over there, by the door!'

Nick and Craig Winters turned to look. At the door of the tea room stood the man with white hair. He looked up and down the room, and then he saw them, and began to walk across to their table. His hand was in his pocket.

For a second or two the three people at the table did not move. Then Craig Winters jumped to his feet. 'That's Mr Hollywood!' he screamed. 'That man there!' And he pointed at Nick.

The man's hand came out of his pocket – with a gun. 'This is for Anna!' he shouted.

*'This is for Anna!' he shouted.*

32

Nick moved very fast. The tea table went over, and Nick was down on the floor in a second. The shot went over his head, and Meg screamed. At the same time Craig Winters shouted out and put a hand on his arm. There was blood on his white shirt. Then more people began to scream, and two waiters pulled the man with white hair down on to the floor.

'Get the police!' somebody shouted.

# — 7 —

## At the police station

It was 7.30 p.m. Nick and Meg were in a room at the police station. The man called Vickers was in a different room, with three detectives. There was a doctor with him too. Craig Winters was at the hospital.

The door opened and a detective came in with two cups of coffee. He put them down on the table, and turned to go out again.

'Detective Edmonds,' Meg said, 'did the hospital call? Is Craig going to be all right?'

'Winters?' Detective Edmonds said. 'Yes, he's going to be OK.'

'Can I call the hospital now?' asked Meg.

'I'd like you to wait,' said Edmonds. 'Detective Keat is going to be here in a minute. He's just coming from the airport and—' He looked through the open door. 'Ah, here he is now.'

A second detective came into the room, and behind him was a tall man with dark hair.

Meg stood up quickly. 'Daddy!' she cried. 'What are you doing here?'

'The police called me,' said Howard Hutson, 'and I flew

here at once. Detective Keat met me at the airport. Now, sit down, Meg. I want you to listen to me.' He did not look at Nick.

Meg sat down and her father took her hands. 'Meg, last week Johnnie Vickers came to my house. He wanted to talk about his daughter. You remember Anna, Meg? Three months ago she jumped off a bridge in Boston and died. She was young, beautiful, rich – and she didn't want to live. Why? Because she loved a man, and the man took her money, ran away and left her. And the man was called—'

'No!' said Meg. 'NO!'

'Yes, Meg, yes. He was called Mr Hollywood.'

'No!' shouted Meg. She began to cry.

'That's right, Miss Hutson,' said detective Keat quietly. 'To you, he gave the name Craig Winters. When Anna Vickers knew him, he was Carl Windser. But he liked all his . . . er . . . girlfriends to call him Mr Hollywood. He took nearly 50,000 dollars from Anna Vickers. And there was a girl before that . . .'

'No, it's not true!' Meg shouted.

'It *is* true, Meg,' said her father. 'Winters – Windser – gets all his money from rich men's daughters. Johnnie Vickers loved his daughter. He went to her house in Boston after she died. He read her letters, and learned about the money and the name Mr Hollywood. And when he came to my house, I told him about you, Meg. I said, "My

35

daughter's got a new boyfriend, and she calls him Mr Hollywood. I don't like him, but I can't stop her. She's going away to meet him next week, I think. What can I do?" Johnnie put his hand on my arm, and he said, "Don't be afraid for your daughter. I'm going to find that man – and stop him!"'

Meg said nothing. Her face was very white. For a minute or two nobody spoke, then detective Edmonds said:

'Vickers told us all about it, Miss Hutson. He followed you to Whistler, and saw you with—'

Nick began to understand. 'With me, in the café! And Meg called me Mr Hollywood!'

Howard Hutson looked at Nick. 'You're the travel writer guy, right?'

'Lortz. Nick Lortz,' said Nick. 'Vickers nearly killed me. He shot at me twice, and—'

But Howard Hutson was not very interested in Nick. He looked at his daughter again.

'How much money did you give him, Meg?' he said.

'I – I gave him 25,000 dollars,' said Meg. 'Only for two or three months, he said. Then he . . .' She began to cry again.

'Well, you can say goodbye to that money,' said Hutson angrily.

'What's going to happen to Vickers?' Nick asked detective Edmonds.

*Meg said nothing.*

'Hospital, I think,' said Edmonds. 'OK, he shot at you and about fifty people saw him. But he's not a well man. The doctors are going to put him away in a hospital.'

Howard Hutson stood up. 'OK, Meg, I'm going to take you home. My plane is waiting at the airport.'

Meg followed her father to the door, then she

37

remembered Nick and turned.

'I'm sorry,' she said. 'I got you into all this. I called you Mr Hollywood. That was wrong. But I didn't know—'

'It's OK,' said Nick. 'You know everything now. And it's better to learn it now, and not later. 50,000 dollars later.'

*'I'm sorry I got you into all this.'*

## — 8 —

## A nice smile

Nick took the evening ferry back to Vancouver. He was tired and hungry, so he went down to get some dinner in the ferry restaurant.

The restaurant was busy and there was only one free table. Nick sat down quickly and began to eat. 'I must get back to work tomorrow,' he thought, 'and forget about millionaires' daughters and men with guns.'

'Excuse me,' somebody said. 'Can I sit with you?'

*'Excuse me. Can I sit with you?'*

39

Nick looked up. There was a pretty girl next to his table. He got up.

'It – it's OK,' he said. 'You can have this table. I don't want it.' And he began to move away.

'Please don't go,' the girl said. 'Stay and finish your dinner.' She smiled at him. It was a nice smile.

But Nick knew all about nice smiles.

'I'm not hungry,' he said.

And he walked quickly out of the restaurant.

# GLOSSARY

**bar**  a room where people can buy and have drinks

**blood**  blood is red and moves around inside the body

**bridge**  something built high to go over a river or a road

**busy**  with many things happening

**café**  a place where people can buy and eat food and drink

**city**  a big important town

**crowd**  a lot of people

**desk**  people in offices sit and work at desks

**fall** (past tense **fell**)  to go down quickly from a high place

**ferry**  a ship to carry cars and people

**floor**  the part of a room which is under your feet

**fly** (past tense **flew**)  to travel through the air (e.g. by aeroplane)

**follow**  to go after someone or something

**great**  wonderful, very good

**guess**  to try to give the right answer when you don't know it

**gun**  a thing that shoots out bullets to kill people

**guy**  a man

**kiss** *(v)*  to touch someone with your lips, to show love, or to say hello or goodbye

**magazine**  a book with a paper cover which comes out every week, month, etc.

**maybe**  perhaps

**millionaire**  somebody who has a million pounds or dollars, or more

**mountain**  a very big hill

**movie**  a film which you see at a cinema

**mystery**  something that you do not understand and cannot explain

**outside**   not in something (a room, a building, etc.)

**park** *(n)*   a garden or place in a town where people can walk, sit, play games, etc.

**party**   a meeting of friends to eat, drink, talk, dance, etc.

**point** *(v)*   to show with your finger where someone or something is

**policeman**   the police are the men and women in a country who catch criminals, try to stop people doing wrong, etc.

**police station**   an office of the police

**pretty**   beautiful, nice to look at

**pull**   to hold and move something towards you

**push**   to move something away from you with your hands

**restaurant**   a place where people can buy and eat meals

**scream**   to cry out loudly, usually when you are afraid or hurt

**shoot** (past tense **shot**)   to send a bullet from a gun to kill or hurt somebody

**short**   not tall

**shot** *(n)*   the bullet sent from a gun

**shout** *(v)*   to call or cry out loudly and strongly

**stranger**   somebody that you do not know

**sure**   certain, knowing that something is true

**tea**   a hot drink, often with sugar and milk or lemon

**travel**   to visit other countries, cities, etc.

**turn**   to move round

**vacation**   a holiday, a time when you do not work and perhaps go travelling

**waiter**   somebody who brings your food or drink in a restaurant or café

**worried**   afraid that something is wrong or something bad is going to happen

# Goodbye, Mr Hollywood

## ACTIVITIES

## *Before Reading*

1 **Read the introduction on the first page of the book, and the back cover. How much do you know now about the story? Tick one of the boxes.**

| | YES | NO |
|---|---|---|
| 1 This is a mystery story. | ☐ | ☐ |
| 2 The story happens in the USA. | ☐ | ☐ |
| 3 Nick gets a kiss from a beautiful girl in a café. | ☐ | ☐ |
| 4 Nick met the girl three weeks ago. | ☐ | ☐ |
| 5 The girl calls Nick 'Mr Hollywood'. | ☐ | ☐ |
| 6 Nick knows the man with short white hair. | ☐ | ☐ |
| 7 When Nick leaves the café, he forgets about the girl. | ☐ | ☐ |

2 **What is going to happen in the story? Can you guess? Tick one box for each sentence.**

| | YES | NO | PERHAPS |
|---|---|---|---|
| 1 Nick tries to find the girl | ☐ | ☐ | ☐ |
| 2 Somebody tries to kill Nick. | ☐ | ☐ | ☐ |
| 3 Nick kills 'Mr Hollywood'. | ☐ | ☐ | ☐ |
| 4 Nick gets a lot of money. | ☐ | ☐ | ☐ |
| 5 Nick meets the man with short white hair. | ☐ | ☐ | ☐ |

## *While Reading*

**Read Chapter 1 and answer these questions.**

1  Who first saw the girl across the street?
2  What did Nick learn from the letter in the girl's bag?
3  The girl knew somebody called 'Mr Hollywood'. Why
   was he called that?
4  Who followed Nick when he left the café?
5  Who watched Nick from a hotel window?

**Read Chapter 2, and then complete these sentences. Use
one word for each gap.**

1  Nick fell in front of a car because somebody _____ him.
2  In the hotel Nick read a _____ and saw a _____ of Jan.
3  She was Meg Hutson, the daughter of a _____.

**Read Chapter 3. Choose the best question-word for these
questions, and then answer them.**

*Who / Where / What*
1  . . . noise did Nick hear in the park?
2  . . . did Nick find on the window of his car?
3  . . . did Nick go next?
4  . . . wrote down Nick's story?

**Read Chapter 4. Are these sentences true (T) or false (F)? Change the false sentences into true ones.**

1 The woman at the hotel desk was not interested in Nick's questions about a man with white hair.
2 It was a very small hotel.
3 Nick remembered the letter in the girl's bag.
4 Nick saw the man with white hair in a taxi.
5 A small girl ran in front of Nick in the hotel restaurant, and Nick ran into her.
6 The name of the man with white hair was Mr Hutson.

**Read Chapter 5, and then put these sentences in the right order.**

1 He saw Nick's car outside the hotel.
2 Nick took the ferry to Vancouver Island.
3 Then he came into the hotel, with a gun in his pocket.
4 She was in the hotel tea room with a man.
5 Then he went to the Empress Hotel in Victoria and asked for Meg Hutson.
6 But the man with white hair followed Nick to Vancouver Island.

**Read Chapter 6. Who said this, and to whom?**

1 'No, thanks. I'm with the two people over there.'
2 'Sometimes called Mr Hollywood?'

3 'I think he's a detective. And I think he's working for my father.'

4 'Tell – tell me about this man with white hair.'

5 'You're afraid of him. Why?'

6 'That's Mr Hollywood! That man there!'

7 'This is for Anna!'

**Before you read Chapters 7 and 8, look at these sentences. Can you guess the best ending for each sentence?**

1 Mr Vickers wants to kill Mr Hollywood because . . .

a) he likes to kill people.

b) Mr Hollywood killed or hurt someone in his family.

c) Mr Hollywood took all his money.

2 Anna is Mr Vickers' . . .

a) daughter.

b) sister.

c) wife.

3 Craig Winters . . .

a) dies.

b) goes to prison.

c) goes to hospital.

4 Mr Vickers . . .

a) dies.

b) goes to prison.

c) goes to hospital.

## After Reading

1 Read this newspaper report about the shooting at the Empress Hotel. There are 16 things wrong with it. Find the mistakes and correct them.

This afternoon a gunman shot a woman in the Empress Hotel in Victoria. 'He walked past me and went into the television room,' said the woman behind the hotel desk. 'He was a short fat man with red hair.'

The man took a gun out of his bag and walked across to a table. A young woman at this table jumped to her feet and shouted, 'Mr Hollywood's not here!' A second young woman pushed over the tea table. The gunman shot three times and hit one of the young women in the leg.

Three waiters pulled the gunman down on to the floor. Soon after, the police arrived.

The gunman is Mr Nick Lortz. His daughter Meg died three months ago in San Francisco. She fell under a train.

Now choose the best headline for the report.

- MAN KILLED AT EMPRESS HOTEL
- SHOOTING AT THE EMPRESS
- WOMAN SHOT BY MYSTERY GUNMAN
- DINNER STOPS FOR GUNMAN

2 **Match the people with the sentences. Then use the sentences to write a short description of each person. Use pronouns (*he, she, him, her*) and linking words (*but, and, because*) when you can.**

*Nick Lortz / Meg Hutson / Craig Winters /*
*Howard Hutson / Johnnie Vickers*

**Example:** *Nick met a girl in a café in Whistler.* **He didn't know her, but he . . .**

1 *Nick* met a girl in a café in Whistler.

2 _____ was the daughter of a millionaire.

3 _____ used a lot of different names.

4 _____ was Meg's father.

5 _____ was the man with white hair.

6 _____ loved a man called Craig Winters.

7 _____ wanted to stop his daughter seeing 'Mr Hollywood'.

8 *Nick* didn't know this girl.

9 _____ got all his money from rich men's daughters.

10 _____ thought that Nick was 'Mr Hollywood'.

11 _____ was happy to sit and talk with this girl.

12 _____ liked his girlfriends to call him 'Mr Hollywood'.

13 _____ gave Craig Winters 25,000 dollars.

14 _____ tried three times to kill Nick.

15 _____ knew Johnnie Vickers.

3 Here is a new illustration for the story. Find the best place
  in the story to put the picture, and answer these questions.

The picture goes on page _____ .

1 Who are the two men in the picture?

2 Where are they?

3 What are they doing?

**Now write a caption for the illustration.**

*Caption:* _____

4 How does Craig Winters get 25,000 dollars out of Meg? Put their telephone conversation in the right order, and write in the names. Craig speaks first (number 5).

1 _____ 'Why? What's the matter?'

2 _____ 'No, no. I can't take money from you, Meg.'

3 _____ 'Craig, I'm fine. But I want to see you. When can we meet?'

4 _____ 'Meg, you're wonderful. How about 25,000? Just for two or three months, you understand.'

5 _____ 'Hi, Meg. How are you?'

6 _____ 'It's my mother. I can't leave her because her legs are very bad and she can't walk far. She needs a new car, but I don't have the money just now.'

7 _____ 'Of course you can! How much do you need? 15,000? 20,000? Just tell me. You can have it tomorrow.'

8 _____ 'I don't know. I want to see you too, but things aren't easy at the moment.'

9 _____ 'But Craig, that's easy! I can give you the money.'

5 Use words from (1) with words from (2) to make some new titles for this story. How many titles can you make? Which ones are best for the story?

1 a / the / at / in / with / of / and / hello

2 café / daughter / girl / hair / Hollywood / man / Mr / meeting / mystery / nice / rich / smile / Whistler / white / Winters / wrong

# ABOUT THE AUTHOR

John Escott worked in business before becoming a writer. Since then he has written many books for readers of all ages, but enjoys writing crime and mystery thrillers most of all. He was born in Somerset, in the west of England, but now lives in Bournemouth on the south coast. When he is not working, he likes looking for long-forgotten books in small back-street bookshops, watching old Hollywood films on video, and walking for miles along empty beaches.

He has written or retold many stories for the Oxford Bookworms Library. His original stories include *Dead Man's Island* and *Agatha Christie, Woman of Mystery* (both at Stage 2).

# ABOUT BOOKWORMS

## OXFORD BOOKWORMS LIBRARY
*Classics • True Stories • Fantasy & Horror • Human Interest*
*Crime & Mystery • Thriller & Adventure*

The OXFORD BOOKWORMS LIBRARY offers a wide range of original and adapted stories, both classic and modern, which take learners from elementary to advanced level through six carefully graded language stages:

| | |
|---|---|
| **Stage 1** (400 headwords) | **Stage 4** (1400 headwords) |
| **Stage 2** (700 headwords) | **Stage 5** (1800 headwords) |
| **Stage 3** (1000 headwords) | **Stage 6** (2500 headwords) |

More than fifty titles are also available on cassette, and there are many titles at Stages 1 to 4 which are specially recommended for younger learners. In addition to the introductions and activities in each Bookworm, resource material includes photocopiable test worksheets and Teacher's Handbooks, which contain advice on running a class library and using cassettes, and the answers for the activities in the books.

---

Several other series are linked to the OXFORD BOOKWORMS LIBRARY. They range from highly illustrated readers for young learners, to playscripts, non-fiction readers, and unsimplified texts for advanced learners.

| | |
|---|---|
| *Oxford Bookworms Starters* | *Oxford Bookworms Factfiles* |
| *Oxford Bookworms Playscripts* | *Oxford Bookworms Collection* |

Details of these series and a full list of all titles in the OXFORD BOOKWORMS LIBRARY can be found in the *Oxford English* catalogues. A selection of titles from the OXFORD BOOKWORMS LIBRARY can be found on the next pages.

# White Death

TIM VICARY

Sarah Harland is nineteen, and she is in prison. At the airport, they find heroin in her bag. So, now she is waiting to go to court. If the court decides that it was her heroin, then she must die.

She says she did not do it. But if she did not, who did? Only two people can help Sarah: her mother, and an old boyfriend who does not love her now. Can they work together? Can they find the real criminal before it is too late?

# The President's Murderer

JENNIFER BASSETT

The President is dead!

A man is running in the night. He is afraid and needs to rest. But there are people behind him – people with lights, and dogs, and guns.

A man is standing in front of a desk. His boss is very angry, and the man is tired and needs to sleep. But first he must find the other man, and bring him back – dead or alive.

Two men: the hunter and the hunted. Which will win and which will lose?

Long live the President!

# Remember Miranda

ROWENA AKINYEMI

Cathy Wilson is driving to Norfolk, to begin her new job with the Harvey family. She is going to look after the two young children, Tim and Susan. Cathy meets the children's father, and their grandmother, and their aunt. She meets Nick, the farmer who lives across the fields. But she doesn't meet Miranda, the children's mother, because Miranda is dead.

She died two years ago, and Cathy cannot learn anything about her. Everybody remembers Miranda, but nobody wants to talk about her . . .

# One-Way Ticket

JENNIFER BASSETT

Tom Walsh had a lot to learn about life. He liked travelling, and he was in no hurry. He liked meeting people, anyone and everyone. He liked the two American girls on the train. They were nice and very friendly. They knew a lot of places. Tom thought they were fun. Tom certainly had a lot to learn about life.

This is a collection of short stories about adventures on trains. Strange, wonderful, and frightening things can happen on trains – and all of them happen here.

# The Monkey's Paw

### W. W. JACOBS

*Retold by Diane Mowat*

Outside, the night is cold and wet. Inside, the White family sits and waits. Where is their visitor?

There is a knock at the door. A man is standing outside in the dark. Their visitor has arrived.

The visitor waits. He has been in India for many years. What has he got? He has brought the hand of a small, dead animal – a monkey's paw.

Outside, in the dark, the visitor smiles and waits for the door to open.

# Dead Man's Island

### JOHN ESCOTT

Mr Ross lives on an island where no visitors come. He stops people from taking photographs of him. He is young and rich, but he looks sad. And there is one room in his house which is always locked.

Carol Sanders and her mother come to the island to work for Mr Ross. Carol soon decides that there is something very strange about Mr Ross. Where did he get his money from? How can a young man buy an island? So she watches, and she listens – and one night she learns what is behind the locked door.